ILLINOIS

ILLINOIS

ALDEN R. CARTER

Franklin Watts
New York/London/Toronto/Sydney/1987
A First Book

Cover photographs courtesy of Shostal

Photographs courtesy of Illinois State Historical Society: pp. 20, 22,
28, 32, 35, 37; Springfield Convention & Visitors Bureau: pp. 31, 88;
Chicago Historical Society: pp. 38, 43, 45, 49, 52, 56, 63, 67;
Chicago Convention and Visitors Bureau: pp. 54, 76;
AP/Wide World Photos: p. 69; UPI/Bettmann Newsphotos: p. 70;
Office of the Mayor, Chicago: p. 72; Caterpillar, Inc.: p. 79;
USDA: pp. 81 (Soil Conservation Service), 82;
Illinois Department of Conservation: p. 86.

Library of Congress Cataloging-in-Publication Data

Carter, Alden R.
Illinois.

(A First book)
Bibliography: p.
Includes index.
Summary: Discusses the history, government, economy,
natural resources, and culture of Illinois.
1.   Illinois—Juvenile literature. [1.   Illinois]
I.   Title.
F541.3.C34   1987   977.3   87-6166
ISBN 0-531-10387-0

CONTENTS

ACKNOWLEDGMENTS

Many thanks to all who helped with *Illinois*,
particularly my agent, Ray Puechner; my editor,
Iris Rosoff; and my friends Don and Georgette Beyer,
Dean Markwardt, Dave Samter, and Sue Babcock.
As always, my wife, Carol, deserves much of the credit.

OTHER BOOKS
BY ALDEN R. CARTER

SUPERCOMPUTERS (with Wayne LeBlanc)
MODERN CHINA
MODERN ELECTRONICS (with Wayne LeBlanc)
RADIO: From Marconi to the Space Age

For my Illinois friends,
Jack and Ginny Duwe and Joe Montana

ILLINOIS

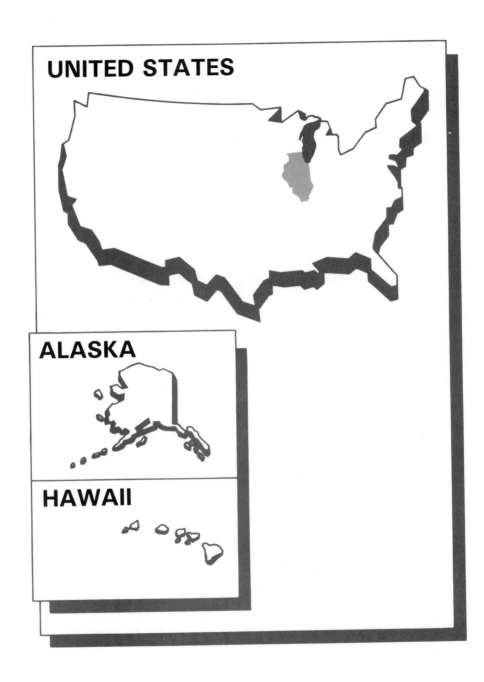

UNITED STATES

ALASKA

HAWAII

1

THE PRAIRIE STATE

Our flight to Chicago takes off from Memphis, Tennessee, on a clear summer afternoon. Below, the wide Mississippi River bustles with barges and pleasure boats. We have been at cruising altitude only a few minutes when another great river, the Ohio, comes into view ahead. The mighty rivers join, and we are flying over Illinois, the dynamic center of America's Midwest.

The Mississippi marks Illinois's western border with Missouri and Iowa. Far ahead of our plane, Wisconsin borders Illinois on the north. To the east lies Indiana and to the southeast Kentucky. In the center, Illinois is shaped like a crude arrowhead, 379 miles (610 km) north to south and 211 miles (340 km) at its widest point. East of the Mississippi, only Georgia has more area. Cairo, Illinois's southernmost city, is on a line with Norfolk, Virginia, while Chicago has the same latitude as Boston, Massachusetts.

Mile after mile, the shadow of our plane sweeps over neat squares and rectangles of cropland. Generations ago, Illinois was nicknamed "the Prairie State" for its great expanses of level grasslands. Today, the prairies have been turned into rich farms. A long growing season and abundant rain make Illinois a leading producer of corn, soybeans, and wheat. Hogs, beef cattle, dairy cows, and sheep are also raised in vast numbers.

THE GIFT OF THE GLACIERS

Illinois's flat, fertile land is a gift left behind by glaciers. Many thousands of years ago, these immense sheets of ice flowed south from

—13

the Arctic. They ground mountains and hills flat and filled valleys and lakes. At least four glaciers covered much of Illinois at various times within the last 250,000 years. In all, some 90 percent of Illinois was affected, and today only Louisiana and Delaware have flatter terrain.

As the climate warmed, the glaciers receded, leaving behind a subsoil of crushed rock. Great windstorms blew as the last glaciers disappeared from Illinois about 15,000 to 25,000 years ago. The winds deposited a rich layer of topsoil. Over the centuries, the wind- and glacier-borne materials combined to give Illinois soil of astonishing fertility.

The water from the melting glaciers formed lakes and rivers. From the air, we can see the many rivers that web the rich farmland of Illinois. About 275 rivers drain the state. Water from twenty-three of the lower forty-eight states flows through Illinois or along its borders on the way to either the Gulf of St. Lawrence or the Gulf of Mexico.

Illinois is blessed not only with fertile soil, but with a wealth of natural resources deeper in the earth. The tropical forests that grew here millions of years ago died, decayed, and were compressed into huge deposits of coal. An estimated two-thirds of the state has minable coal deposits, giving Illinois the largest coal reserves east of the Mississippi.

Deposits of oil, natural gas, fluorspar, lead, iron ore, and silver are also found in the state. Beds of sand, gravel, stone, limestone, and clay are mined for the production of bricks, concrete, and tile.

A VAST TRANSPORTATION NETWORK

As we cross the middle of the state east of the state capital at Springfield, we can see the extensive system of highways and railroads crisscrossing the land. It is difficult to find a better-developed transportation network anywhere.

The web of highways and railroads tightens as our plane banks and begins its descent toward the great metropolis of Chicago, the transportation hub of the Midwest. Night is falling, and the lights of the industrial cities of northern Illinois wink below. In a few minutes, we are over the suburbs of Chicago, America's third largest city.

Busy O'Hare Field is clogged with incoming flights, so we swing out over the broad expanse of Lake Michigan. The shipping channels leading to and from America's largest inland port are busy this evening. Heavily laden lake freighters plow toward Chicago with cargoes of iron ore and other raw materials. Other ships are outbound for such destinations as Detroit, Cleveland, and Buffalo. Some of these ships are oceangoing vessels beginning the passage across the Great Lakes to the St. Lawrence Seaway, the Atlantic Ocean, and the far corners of the earth.

As we swing back inland, we receive landing permission. We start our final approach. On all sides, the broad avenues and quiet residential streets of Chicago glitter in the falling dark. About three million people live in Chicago, and the metropolitan area is home to over seven million. We touch down, the engines reverse, and the plane is soon taxiing toward the main terminal of the busiest airport in the world.

It is difficult to imagine that not very long ago Chicago did not exist, a third of Illinois was covered with forest, and the great prairies grew only grass. Illinois residents were Indians who hunted deer and buffalo, fished the streams, gathered wild plants, and farmed small plots as they had for generations. But just as the glaciers had shaped the land, the arrival of Europeans would change the face of Illinois forever.

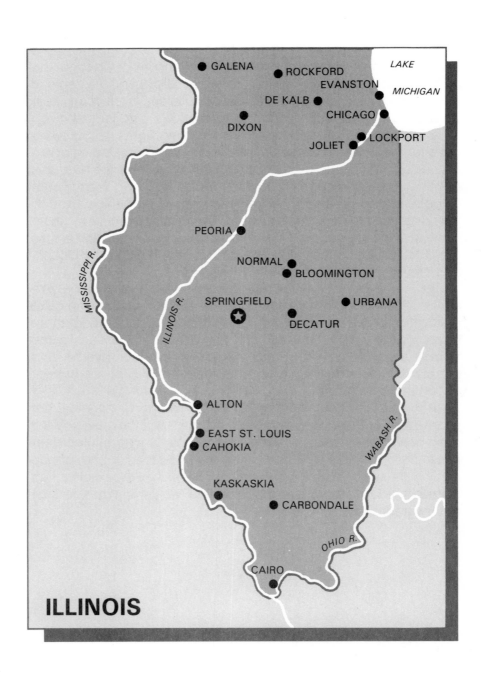

GALENA

ROCKFORD

EVANSTON

LAKE

MICHIGAN

DE KALB

CHICAGO

DIXON

JOLIET

LOCKPORT

MISSISSIPPI R.

PEORIA

NORMAL

BLOOMINGTON

ILLINOIS R.

SPRINGFIELD

URBANA

DECATUR

ALTON

WABASH R.

EAST ST. LOUIS

CAHOKIA

KASKASKIA

CARBONDALE

OHIO R.

CAIRO

ILLINOIS

INDIANS, TRADERS,
AND SETTLERS

In the age of the last glaciers, a land bridge spanned the Bering Strait between Asia and Alaska. At least twenty-five thousand years ago, the ancestors of modern Indians began crossing the bridge to North America. About ten thousand years ago, some of these Paleo-Indians (paleo means early) drifted into what is now Illinois. They were nomads, often on the move in search of game and edible plants.

The richness of Illinois made frequent movement less necessary. Later generations established a routine of migrating between seasonal campgrounds, returning to the same sites year after year. Archaeologists have explored some of these ancient camps, finding spear points, stones used to grind grain, and evidence of woven baskets.

THE FIRST VILLAGES

Around 2,000 B.C., the ancient peoples of Illinois began to build villages. They learned to cultivate plants and make pottery. Village life required a more orderly society, and complex social systems and religious rites developed.

Civilization in Illinois reached a peak between 500 B.C. and A.D. 500 with a culture scientists call the Hopewell. The Hopewellians lived in large villages, practiced agriculture and skilled crafts, traded widely, and buried their dead in large mounds. For reasons no one completely understands, the Hopewell culture eventually disappeared.

Several hundred years later, another civilization called the Middle Mississippian rose along the major rivers of Illinois. Known popularly as the Mound Builders, they raised huge earthworks and built temples and houses for their priests on the level tops. Many of these "mounds" can be visited today. The largest is near East St. Louis. Monks' Mound is 100 feet (30 m) tall, 710 feet (216 m) wide, and 1,080 feet (329 m) long. In all, it covers a spectacular seventeen acres (6.9 hectares).

Around the time of Columbus, the Middle Mississippian culture collapsed. Some scientists suggest that diseases brought by the first European explorers may have spread inland to doom the inhabitants. The Indians who succeeded the Mound Builders followed a simpler way of life. They cultivated some plants and lived at least part of the year in small villages. These Indians called themselves Iliniwek, a word meaning "the men" that implied that non-Iliniwek were inferior.

THE ARRIVAL OF EUROPEANS

We do not know the identity of the first European to enter what is now Illinois. He was almost certainly a French fur trader. Either alone or with an Indian guide, he had probably followed the shoreline of Lake Michigan south from Canada to reach Illinois. Even if he could read and write, he was uninterested in history and left no written account. His interest was trade, and his canoe carried a cargo of European goods to exchange for furs.

We also do not know the reaction of the first Iliniwek in seeing a white person. He or she was probably not as shocked as we might suppose. The Indians of Illinois had heard of white people from tribes further to the east. Most likely, the Indians were anxious to begin trading for the wondrous products of European civilization.

FRANCE SENDS EXPLORERS

The Indians gave Illinois's first official explorers a friendly greeting. The explorers had been sent south by the French governor of Canada to investigate rumors of a great river flowing west to the Pacific. In command of the small expedition was a daring young Frenchman, Louis Jolliet. Traveling with him was Jacques Marquette, a Jesuit missionary more interested in converting the Indians than finding an easy water route to the Orient.

The explorers crossed Lake Michigan and followed the Fox and Wisconsin rivers to the Mississippi. On about June 20, 1673, they paddled their birchbark canoes into what is now Illinois. They were awed by the prairies and the great herds of buffalo along the Mississippi banks. It became obvious, however, that the river did not flow into the Pacific Ocean, but into the Gulf of Mexico instead. Near the mouth of the Ohio River, the explorers turned back. On the advice of friendly Indians, they followed the Illinois and Des Plaines rivers across the land of the Iliniwek. The French would name the land Illinois, a combination of the first two syllables of Iliniwek and the French ending "ois."

At the head of the Des Plaines, the explorers carried their equipment across a strip of low land to the Chicago River, which emptied into Lake Michigan a few miles away. With great foresight, Jolliet predicted that the easy portage linking the Great Lakes and the Mississippi River system would have immense value in the future. Within two centuries, one of the world's great cities, Chicago, would stand on the site. (The original meaning of the word Chicago is disputed. Some scholars maintain that it is derived from the Iliniwek word for "great"; others argue that the Indian word meant "wild onions.")

Marquette and Jolliet parted at Green Bay in what is now Wisconsin. Jolliet pushed on toward Montreal to deliver his report. Marquette returned to Illinois and established a mission at an Indian village near present-day Ottawa in north-central Illinois. In poor

*Father Jacques Marquette and Louis Jolliet
discover the Mississippi.*

health, the courageous priest attempted to return to Canada in 1675, but died on the way. Other Jesuits replaced him in Illinois.

FRENCH SETTLEMENT

Other French explorers soon arrived in the Illinois country. A young French nobleman, Robert Cavelier, Sieur de la Salle, and Henri de Tonti, a professional soldier of Italian birth, spent several years trying to establish forts and trading posts in Illinois. Exploring further south, they reached the mouth of the Mississippi in 1682 and claimed the vast lands drained by the river for France. However, the French government gave their ambitious plans little support.

After La Salle's early death, Henri de Tonti continued the settlement effort for thirteen years. Eventually, Tonti and his missionary allies established a more or less permanent series of outposts along the long westward bend of the Mississippi across from where St. Louis now stands. Cahokia, now part of East St. Louis, is the oldest permanent settlement in Illinois. A short distance south, Kaskaskia was established in 1703 and remained for more than a century Illinois's most important town.

The French settlements stayed small. In the next half century, the total population of the river villages never exceeded 2,000 whites and perhaps 600 black and Indian slaves. Life was peaceful. The local Indian tribes were friendly, and many Frenchmen chose Indian wives. The rich bottomland made farming easy. The settlements shipped cargoes of flour, tallow, bacon, lead, and lumber downriver to New Orleans.

BRITAIN'S SHORT RULE

Because of their isolation and small population, the river villages played little part in a long series of wars fought between France and Britain from 1689 to 1763. In 1759 the British captured the French stronghold at Quebec, ending France's long rule in Canada.

Illinois became part of the British Empire. A small British garrison arrived at Fort de Chartres, upriver from Kaskaskia, in 1765.

Meanwhile, the British government had decided to forbid settlement west of the Allegheny Mountains. Many American pioneers chose to ignore the rule and a few American traders trekked as far inland as Illinois.

The settlement ban was one of many issues that led to the outbreak of the American Revolution in 1775. War on the frontier was brutal. The British recruited Indians to raid villages and lone cabins. The Indians, already disturbed by the spread of white settlement, happily obliged. The British military governor of Detroit, Lt. Col. Henry Hamilton, was accused by the colonists of paying a bounty on all scalps, no matter what the age or sex of the original owner.

AMERICAN VICTORY
IN THE WEST

The American Revolution came to Illinois in July 1778 when a rugged Virginian, George Rogers Clark, led a small army into Kaskaskia. The local garrison quickly surrendered. Clark learned from sympathetic French residents that the important town of Vincennes across the Wabash River lay undefended. He sent a small detachment to take control.

Hamilton easily retook Vincennes in the fall. Thinking the fighting was over for the year, he dismissed his Indian allies. In a daring march, Clark led his troops across the Illinois wilderness of frozen woods and flooded swamps. On February 23, 1779, Clark surprised the garrison at Vincennes. Two days later, Hamilton surrendered.

Robert Cavelier, Sieur de la Salle, explored in Illinois.

Without the troops and supplies to take Detroit, Clark was forced to be on the defensive for the rest of the war. However, when peace talks opened after the American victory at Yorktown in 1781, Clark's exploits allowed American negotiators to claim "the old Northwest"—the vast territory that would become Illinois, Ohio, Indiana, Michigan, Wisconsin, and part of Minnesota. Surprisingly, the British negotiators readily agreed. Perhaps never in history had so much potential wealth been signed away so casually.

BUILDING AN EMPIRE
IN MID-AMERICA

Before the end of the Revolution, English-speaking settlers began arriving in the old French villages. The rich bottomland between the present-day cities of Alton and Chester became known as American Bottom to distinguish it from the settled strip of land on the west side of the river in Spanish territory.

The first English-speaking settlers were mostly poor, rural southerners. They were a restless, rough, independent people. They cared little for government, and more than a few had brushed against the wrong side of the law further east. At first, the population of Illinois grew slowly. The arrival of the new settlers was offset by the migration of French residents to St. Louis in Spanish-held territory. A census in 1800 recorded only 2,458 white people in Illinois, about the same number there had been fifty years earlier.

THE HARD PIONEER LIFE

The next decade saw a rapid increase in settlement. Most of the arrivals from the East were young married couples, who brought only a few tools and the stamina to survive in the wilderness. They usually chose land along the wooded banks of a southern-Illinois river. They mistakenly believed that prairie land was infertile because it didn't support trees. As settlements expanded in the southern third of Illinois, the area became known as Egypt, for reasons now forgotten.

The pioneer homestead rarely amounted to more than ten acres (four hectares) of cleared land and a small log cabin. A few acres of corn, a garden, a few hogs, and a cow made the pioneer family self-sufficient. The plentiful game in the surrounding woods added fresh meat to the diet. Clothing was usually made at home from deerskin or homespun wool.

Families were large, averaging ten children. A family could expect to lose two or three children in the first five years of life to smallpox, cholera, typhoid, pneumonia, or one of the other diseases that thrived in Egypt. Children who survived the dangerous early years of life went to work in the fields or around the house as soon as they were able. Schools did not exist, and the highest educational achievement of most people was the ability to sign a crude signature.

Yet, not all was hard work and misery for the pioneers. Most families had numerous relatives living nearby. Visits, weddings, and house-raisings were happy occasions. The climate was agreeable most of the year, and many a youngster slipped away from chores to while away an afternoon hunting or fishing.

THE EDUCATED FEW

Life on the frontier attracted more than simple country folk. Ambitious, well-educated people began arriving to start businesses and law practices. They quickly became the community leaders. Almost all of them speculated in land, buying as much as they could in the hope that future development would make them rich.

In 1803 the United States undertook the largest—and probably the smartest—land speculation in history. The French dictator Napoleon Bonaparte had recovered the vast lands west of the Mississippi from Spain. He sold them to the United States for fifteen million dollars, a deal that doubled the area of the new nation. Illinois no longer sat on the western frontier of the country, but in the middle.

Illinois was part of Indiana Territory, which also included all or part of present-day Wisconsin, Indiana, Minnesota, and Michigan. The seat of government was in Vincennes. Illinois leaders demanded a capital closer to the settled area along the Mississippi. In 1808 Congress responded by creating the Territory of Illinois with a capital at Kaskaskia. Illinois Territory covered two and a half times the area of today's Illinois—much of it the unmapped wilderness of Wisconsin and upper Minnesota.

INDIAN ANGER GROWS

The Indians watched the settlement of their land with increasing alarm. The whites were overhunting the land, claiming traditional campgrounds as their own, and frequently cheating the Indians with shoddy trade goods. Ironically, the inevitable confrontation would happen in a place where white/Indian relations had been good.

In the early years of the century, the Chicago Portage had a few homes and the trading post built about 1779 by Chicago's first non-Indian resident, Jean Baptiste Point DuSable, a black or mulatto from the West Indies. Fur trading had made DuSable reasonably well-off, and he sold his business and moved on in 1800.

In 1803 American troops arrived to build Fort Dearborn. The garrison got on well with the Indians until 1811, when an Indian uprising in Indiana was crushed at the Battle of Tippecanoe. Resentful and frustrated, the Indians of the area were joyous when war broke out between Britain and the United States in 1812.

A British force from Canada soon threatened American forts on the Great Lakes. The American commander at Detroit panicked and ordered the evacuation of Fort Dearborn. Against the advice of his Indian experts, the post's commander complied. On a clear, hot morning in August, he marched his soldiers and their families out of the fort. Almost immediately Indians attacked the column. The fight was quick and savage. In all, about seventy-five white men,

women, and children were slaughtered. A few were rescued by friendly Indians or carried into captivity.

News of the massacre enraged the white population of southern Illinois. Militia expeditions attacked Indian villages whose inhabitants had no connection with the massacre. When Britain and the United States made peace in 1814, the situation calmed, but white fear did not die. Soon demands were being made for the eviction of all Indians from Illinois.

The Indians rapidly lost title to their lands. Congress granted 160-acre (65-hectare) plots in Illinois to veterans of the War of 1812. Most veterans sold their land to speculators in the East. About the same time, surveyors finished mapping Illinois, and large blocks of government land went on sale at a minimum price of $2—later lowered to $1.25—an acre (.4 hectare). By 1818 the tribes of Illinois were doomed. The government—often in negotiation with Indians who did not speak for their tribes—had purchased most of the land and was busily selling it off.

STATEHOOD

As Illinois grew, territorial government became less satisfactory. The Northwest Ordinance of 1797 had outlined the procedure for creating new states in the Great Lakes region. The minimum population had been set at 60,000, but the Illinois representative to Congress got that reduced to 40,000. Some creative counting was required to reach even that number—the real population was closer to 35,000—but Congress accepted the census.

A state constitution was quickly drawn, and Illinois became the twenty-first state on December 3, 1818. Kaskaskia was the first

Jean Baptiste Point DuSable was Chicago's first non-Indian resident.

capital. In 1820 the legislature moved to Vandalia, a new town eighty miles (129 km) northwest, where the land-speculating legislators sought to spur new development. The capital would be moved to its present site at Springfield in 1840.

IMMIGRANTS FROM THE NORTHEAST

In 1820 Illinois was still a frontier state. (Kaskaskia, the biggest town, had fewer than two hundred houses.) New immigrants would change that. In the next ten years the population of Illinois would nearly triple, then nearly triple again by 1840. By mid-century, Illinois would be the fastest-growing state in the nation.

The Indians made one more attempt to halt the flood, but the pathetic Black Hawk War of 1832 only led to the final eviction of the Indians. By the mid-1830s, no significant Indian population existed in Illinois.

The majority of the new arrivals in Illinois came from the Northeast instead of the South. Many were better educated and more open to new ideas than the earlier arrivals. While the southerners had avoided the treeless prairie, the northerners set about testing its fertility. The heavy sod and the wide expanses of the prairie required new farming tools. The wooden plow was replaced by the cast-iron plow. In 1837 an Illinois blacksmith, John Deere, invented an even better plow with a blade of steel.

The steel plow pulled easier than earlier plows, and farmers began replacing oxen with draft horses. Inventors designed a wide

The old state capitol in Springfield. It was here on June 16, 1858, that Lincoln delivered his famous "House Divided" speech.

variety of horse-drawn machines. The most famous was the grain reaper perfected by Cyrus McCormick. In an hour or two, a McCormick reaper could cut as much grain as a farmer with a scythe could harvest in a whole day.

The new generation of labor-saving equipment produced a spectacular increase in cultivated land. By 1850, 500,000 acres (202,500 hectares) of Illinois were "under the plow." By 1860, the figure would reach 13,291,000 acres (5,382,900 hectares), nearly two-thirds of the land suitable for farming.

BETTER TRANSPORTATION

Another invention, the steamboat, revolutionized water transportation. The first steamboats began appearing on the Mississippi shortly before 1820. Within a few years, they were a common sight on the Mississippi, Ohio, Wabash, and Illinois rivers. Deeper draft vessels combining sail and steam began plying the Great Lakes. Illinois shipped grain, whiskey, furs, beeswax, hides, tallow, and many other products by steamboat.

Steamboating was particularly important to the lead-mining region centered at Galena in the northwest corner of the state. The lead had been discovered by the Indians, noted by French explorers, and mined on a small and irregular basis in the 1700s. In the 1820s it produced America's first mining boom. As many as ten thousand miners worked in the lead-producing area extending into Wisconsin and Iowa. Galena was briefly Illinois's most important town.

Water routes and a few score miles of often muddy roads were no longer enough. Illinois's population was growing fast as immi-

A public test of Cyrus McCormick's reaper

grants from northern Europe joined the tide. The state government began improving roads and encouraging the drainage of low areas.

A CANAL AT CHICAGO

The government was soon involved in another transportation project: a canal across the Chicago Portage to connect the Great Lakes with the Mississippi River system. In 1827, Congress authorized the construction of the canal. The canal commission laid out a town with forty-eight blocks and began selling lots. The village of Chicago was chartered in 1833 with a population of 150. Four years later, more than 4,000 called Chicago home.

Nearly everyone badly underestimated the cost and difficulties of building the canal. The upper reaches of the Des Plaines River were too shallow for barges and had to be bypassed. A canal would have to stretch 96 miles (155 km) from Bridgeport, southwest of Chicago, to La Salle on the Illinois River. Nevertheless, construction began in 1836. One speaker at the celebration that day predicted that Chicago would grow to 100,000 people in a century. Reportedly, members of the crowd doused him with a barrel of water in hopes he would regain his senses.

Irish laborers dug the canal with black powder, horses, shovels, and strong backs. Finally completed in 1848, the canal made Chicago the most important city in Illinois. The arrival of the railroads would make Chicago one of the most important cities in North America.

THE COMING OF
THE RAILROADS

With the canal and its harbor on Lake Michigan, Chicago became the hub of railroad development in Illinois. Besides natural advantages, Chicago also had clever promoters and "the little giant," Senator Stephen A. Douglas, Illinois's most influential politician.

*The canal connecting the Great Lakes
with the Mississippi River made Chicago
the most important city in the state.*

The state had botched an attempt to build railroads in the 1830s. Now it was private enterprise's turn. Starting in 1848, the tycoon William B. Ogden built the first successful railroad out of Chicago, the Galena and Chicago Union. Soon other companies were pushing tracks across the Prairie State.

Meanwhile, Senator Douglas was dreaming big. He wanted a railroad from the Gulf of Mexico to Chicago. To underwrite construction expenses, he persuaded Congress to transfer millions of acres of federal land to the states. Illinois's share alone amounted to 2,595,000 acres (1,051,000 hectares).

Along the right-of-ways granted by the state, the Illinois Central sold farmland and plotted towns. Often immigrants stepped from trains to find only a station and surveyors' stakes standing in the broad, unsettled prairie. Few of the arrivals got back on board; most stayed to farm and build.

The railroad network expanded with almost breathtaking speed. The first railroad from the East reached the city in 1852, arriving on the heels of two other new inventions, the telegraph and the gas streetlight. By 1857, eleven main lines ran into Chicago.

Rough and sprawling, Chicago was becoming a great city almost overnight. New factories, including the huge McCormick reaper plant, called for workers. The stacks of giant ironworks began belching smoke into the prairie sky. Packing plants and stockyards opened to process the great herds of cattle being raised on the Illinois prairies. Illinois was soon the nation's leading grain producer, and huge grain elevators rose along the skyline of Chicago.

By 1860, 3,000 factories were operating in Chicago. The city's population had topped 110,000, making it the ninth largest city in the country. The daily arrival of trains filled with immigrants had

Stephen A. Douglas was one of Illinois's most influential politicians.

*The Chicago stockyards
in the early twentieth century*

swelled the population of Illinois to over 1,700,000, fourth in the Union. Nearly 550,000 were children of school age. A decade before, less than one child in three had attended school. By 1860, Illinois supported 9,162 schools enrolling 86 percent of Illinois's children.

Few Illinoisans remembered the rude frontier days of forty years before. Their minds were fixed on a future clouded by an impending national crisis: the American Civil War.

WAR, FIRE,
AND REBIRTH

The presidential election of 1860 was the most important in the history of the young nation. The issue of slavery divided the North and South, and civil war threatened. Two of the four presidential candidates were Illinoisans. Stephen A. Douglas, the prominent senator, represented the northern half of a split Democratic party. Abraham Lincoln, a former congressman, carried the hopes of the new Republican party.

Lincoln and Douglas knew each other well. They had run for the same Senate seat in 1858, arguing the slavery issue in a famous series of debates in Illinois. Both men were morally opposed to slavery, but Douglas was willing to allow new states a choice on the issue. Lincoln favored restricting slavery to the South and eliminating it altogether as soon as possible. Although Douglas had won reelection to the Senate, the debates propelled Lincoln into national prominence.

In the 1860 presidential election, Lincoln polled a minority of the popular votes, but won enough electoral votes to become the sixteenth president. Although he wanted to avoid civil war, his election was a signal for southern states to break away from the Union. Douglas promised the new president his full support when the Civil War broke out four days after the inauguration. Within a year, Douglas was stricken with typhoid and died, a great loss for Illinois and the imperiled Union.

THE CIVIL WAR

Over a quarter-million sons of Illinois fought in the war. A number of courageous women served as nurses and relief workers. However, support for the war was not universal in Illinois, where strong ties to the South had existed for generations. As defeat followed defeat for the North, opposition to the war grew, sometimes breaking into open conflict in southern Illinois counties.

Lincoln held firm in his resolve to save the Union. Fortunately, he found a general, Ulysses S. Grant, who could win battles and who had briefly been a resident of Galena. Grant understood that the Civil War was a new kind of conflict: a war where railroads, factories, and sheer numbers often meant more than a general's skill on the battlefield. Grant hammered at the Confederate army until it finally surrendered in the spring of 1865. The most costly war in American history took the lives of some thirty-five thousand men from Illinois, including its first president. In his hour of victory, Lincoln was assassinated.

Illinois emerged from the war stronger than ever. Wartime spending and factory construction had vastly increased its industrial might. (About 6,000 buildings were constructed in Chicago during 1864 alone.) In the country, farmers had adopted labor-saving machinery to replace the men lost to the army. As immigrants poured into the state, Illinois began a new era of phenomenal growth. Like a gigantic steam locomotive gaining speed with every mile, Illinois hurtled through the closing decades of the century.

THE NEW IMMIGRANTS

Grim conditions in Europe and a shortage of jobs in the East motivated many people to head for Illinois. Before the war, foreign immigrants had come largely from Germany, Scandinavia, England, and Ireland. Soon their numbers swelled with immigrants from eastern and southern Europe, including Russia, Lithuania, Poland, Hun-

*The immigrants of Chicago
lived in neighborhoods like this.*

gary, Italy, Greece, and the Balkan countries. With their different languages, customs, and skills, the immigrants gave Illinois a new diversity. The variety of cultures could be seen most easily in Chicago, as the onetime trading post nearly tripled in population between 1860 and 1871.

THE CHICAGO FIRE

Chicago's 300,000 people were jammed into a city that had been built so rapidly that little attention had been paid to safety. Most of its homes, businesses, sidewalks, docks, grain elevators, and even many of its streets were made of wood. Roofs were surfaced with wooden shingles, pitch, felt, and tar. Inflammables such as lumber, hay, firewood, oil, and paint lay stored in buildings across the city. Chicago was an immense firetrap waiting for a spark.

In the dry summer and fall of 1871, fires broke out frequently. Chicago's undermanned, ill-equipped, and overworked fire department fought them with skill and bravery. On the evening of October 8, the firemen confronted a blaze that nothing could stop.

The fire started on the West Side in a barn owned by the O'Leary family. (Mrs. O'Leary was asleep, and the famous story of a cow kicking over a lamp is fiction.) The fire spread quickly to surrounding buildings. Firefighters arrived a few critical minutes late because of a communications error. A strong wind scattered sparks and burning shingles over the neighborhood. By midnight, twenty blocks were ablaze. The fire was out of control and much of Chicago doomed.

Few events in American history contain so many stories of human courage as the Chicago fire. Countless people risked their lives to help family, neighbors, strangers, and even tethered horses.

The Chicago fire of 1871 devastated the city.

The city's thousands huddled in parks and undeveloped areas to watch their city burn.

No disaster in the nation's history so devastated a city. By the following evening when rains cooled the fire, a one-by-three-mile (2-by-5-km) area in the heart of the city lay flattened. About 18,000 buildings had disappeared, 300 people were dead and another 100,000 homeless, and $250,000,000 worth of property had gone up in smoke. But courage and ambition had survived. The editor of the Chicago *Tribune* announced the sentiment: "We have lost money, but we have saved life, health, and vigor. Chicago will rise again."

And rise it did. With courage, determination, and extraordinary generosity and good humor, the people of Chicago set about rebuilding the "Gem of the Prairie." Banks, newspapers, and many businesses reopened within days, their new headquarters often mere shacks. By year's end, a dazzling new Chicago was rising from the ashes.

Before the fire, Chicago had been a city of hastily constructed buildings. The wooden buildings of the former Chicago were replaced with new structures of brick. Streets were widened and paved, the fire department modernized, and a tough fire-prevention code enacted. What had been a bloated frontier town became a sturdy modern city.

THE LABOR MOVEMENT

A decade after the fire, working men and women could look at the rebuilt Chicago with pride. The burned-out shells in the business district had long since been replaced with far grander buildings. Hundreds of new factories drew workers from the city's half-million residents.

Outside Chicago, factories in a score of thriving cities contributed to the economy of the Prairie State. Farm, mine, and industrial products sped to market on a railroad system with about 8,000 miles (13,000 km) of track, half of it laid in the 1870s. The muscle and sweat of the working class had built an empire in Illinois. But what did working people have to show for it? In many cases the answer was simple: not enough.

The most dissatisfied were factory workers, the lower-paid railroad men, and Illinois's increasing number of miners. All worked long hours for scant wages under frequently dangerous conditions. If the economy slowed, owners slashed wages and payrolls. Without unemployment insurance or welfare, laid-off workers and their families sank into poverty.

In the 1880s large numbers of workers started banding together in unions to negotiate—and strike if necessary—for better conditions and higher wages. Most industrialists refused to listen to their employees. Strikes were answered with lockouts and the hiring of strikebreakers from Illinois's large population of unemployed. When strikes turned violent, city and state officials sent the police and the militia to protect the factories, railroads, and mines. The labor movement would win few victories until the twentieth century, while suffering dozens of defeats and hundreds of dead. Still, it survived, eventually winning a better life for the working class.

WOMEN ORGANIZE

Women also began organizing in the decades before the turn of the century. The suffrage movement sought the vote for women. Many Illinois women played active roles in the long struggle. In 1913, women would gain the right to vote in Illinois state elections. In 1920, the United States Constitution would be amended to give the vote to all women.

A second cause that attracted large numbers of women was the temperance movement, which sought to restrict the consumption of alcoholic beverages. The movement maintained—not without cause—that drinking promoted poverty, despair, and immoral behavior. For proof, temperance leaders often pointed to wide-open

Chicago with its slums, crime, and thousands of taverns, brothels, and gambling houses.

THE MAGNIFICENT
JANE ADDAMS

An Illinois woman who fought the terrible conditions in the slums became an inspiration for countless people in many nations. Jane Addams, the daughter of a well-to-do family, moved to the West Side slums of Chicago in 1889. There she founded Hull House to help the poor and uneducated. Eventually, Hull House provided a nursery, schools for children and adults, playgrounds, a community center, and numerous other services. Addams and her colleagues helped slum-dwellers organize to demand better government services and the reform of labor laws.

Addams became internationally known through her books and speeches. She provided a moral example of such force that even corrupt or lazy government officials were often shamed into action. In 1931 Jane Addams became the first American woman to receive the Nobel Peace Prize.

THE GRAY WOLVES

Reformers like Jane Addams were few and crooked officials numerous. Officials took bribes to overlook violations of the law, to grant licenses, and to support special-interest legislation. In Chicago, a group of notoriously corrupt city councilmen became known as the "gray wolves." Patronage, the practice of giving government

Jane Addams, an inspiration to generations, won the Nobel Peace Prize in 1931.

jobs to political foot soldiers who rounded up votes, insured their reelection term after term.

Not all officials were tainted. Carter Harrison, Sr., and later his son served Chicago well as mayors. Governor John Peter Altgeld made courageous stands in favor of education, labor reform, better police courts, and higher taxes on corporations.

Still, corruption in government became so widespread that even the most upright public servants had to compromise with "gray wolves" or crooked legislators. Reform groups would have some success in the first years of the new century, but political corruption—particularly in Chicago—has troubled Illinois politics down to the present.

PROGRESS AND MORE PROGRESS

Growth continued at an amazing rate as Illinois entered the 1890s. With four million residents in 1890, Illinois trailed only Pennsylvania and New York in population. Chicago's population had more than doubled in ten years to over a million, second only to New York City's.

Scientific progress had worked changes in country and city alike. Across what had been largely wilderness half a century before, Illinois farmers had spread a carpet of cultivated fields. Drainage of low-lying land was adding more precious acres. Giant steam-powered farm machines now worked alongside draft horses and McCormick reapers.

Chicago had become one of the most modern cities anywhere with electric lights and telephones. In the business district, the world's first skyscrapers—buildings with interior iron and steel frameworks covered with masonry skins—soared to the unbelievable height of ten and even twelve stories.

Expanding Chicago had become a workshop for an adventurous

group of architects who were rethinking all aspects of building and city design. Louis Sullivan and his even more famous pupil Frank Lloyd Wright became the leaders of the "Chicago School." They pioneered the use of steel girders, poured concrete, fireproofing, and many techniques that would give cities across the nation a modern look. Daniel Burnham not only built skyscrapers, but planned the renovation of entire cities, including Chicago, Cleveland, Baltimore, San Francisco, and Washington, D. C.

THE COLUMBIAN EXPOSITION

Illinois and its great city had become a center of commerce and the arts. It was time for a grand party, a chance to show off to the world. Chicago outbid other cities for the right to hold America's celebration of the four-hundredth anniversary of Columbus's arrival in the New World. Burnham drew the plans, and workmen converted marshy Jackson Park into a brilliantly lit wonderland of fountains, lagoons, boardwalks, and shining white buildings. Promoters claimed that the Manufacturers and Liberal Arts Building was the largest structure in the world with a seating capacity of 300,000.

The World's Columbian Exposition opened on May 1, 1893. Seventy-two foreign countries and nearly all the states in the Union had exhibits. Almost every wonder of modern technology could be found within the 633-acre (256-hectare) exposition site. For most visitors, nothing was more wonderful than the first Ferris wheel with its thirty-six sixty-person cars revolving on a 250-foot (76 m) wheel. Away from the exposition site, visitors gawked at the wonders of downtown Chicago, particularly the twenty-one-story Masonic Temple—the tallest building in the world at the time.

Over 27 million people visited the exposition during its six-month existence. Few came away unimpressed. No longer could anyone fairly say that Chicago was an overgrown village, or that Illinois was any less productive or progressive than the states of the East.

A NEW CENTURY

Like the bold speaker who had been doused in 1836 for predicting a Chicago of 100,000 people, most of the speakers at the exposition were too conservative in their predictions for the future. In twenty years, the technological wonders of the Columbian Exposition would seem hopelessly outmoded, and Illinois and the world would have changed beyond imagining.

No invention had greater impact than the automobile. In 1908 Henry Ford introduced the first of fifteen million Model T's, bringing a reliable, cheap, and durable car within the reach of the average family. By 1916 Illinois had 340,000 automobiles. The Model T opened a wider world for millions in rural America. An Illinois farm couple could bypass the nearby village and drive to a big city. What they bought or observed in the city modernized life back home. Before long, gasoline-powered tractors and trucks became essential tools for the up-to-date farmer. Over the course of the next few decades, the ease of automobile travel would undermine the importance of many small towns, and some would disappear altogether.

City-dwellers were on the move too. In the 1890s electric streetcars replaced cable and horse-drawn streetcars in Chicago. An elevated train line—the celebrated "El"—circled through downtown, already known as the "Loop" after the earlier cable-car route. City transportation further improved when Samuel Insull, the electric utilities tycoon, took control of the system and combined a number of individual lines into a single metropolitan system.

The improved urban transit system and an interurban train system built by Insull promoted the growth of outlying areas. It became

Some of the buildings at
the World's Columbian Exposition

possible for a city worker to move his family to more pleasant surroundings on the outskirts and commute daily to work. Chicago's ethnic neighborhoods and customs began to break down as more and more people moved away from the inner city.

FIGHTING THE MUCK

As the number of motorists increased, no politician could ignore complaints about the state's miserable roads. With a plan to "pull Illinois out of the mud," the government started paving thousands of miles of road. Unfortunately, eliminating one kind of muck led to another.

Large public-works projects gave crooked politicians opportunities for widespread corruption. Perhaps the worst example was the Chicago Sanitary District with its large work force of political appointees, many of whom did little or nothing for their pay. (Despite the corruption, the district did valuable work, ushering in the new century by reversing the flow of the Chicago River to take sewage away from the source of Chicago's drinking water in Lake Michigan. Typhoid deaths fell almost immediately from two thousand a year to a mere fraction of the number.)

Reform forces aided by "muckraking" journalists worked to clean up government. In 1905 most state employees came under a new civil service law that based employment on competence rather than political ties. Laws to improve safety in the workplace and the quality of consumer products passed the legislature under pressure from the growing unions. *The Jungle,* a book by Upton Sinclair which vividly describes the awful conditions in Chicago's mammoth Union Stockyards, helped pass a federal meat-inspection law.

The famous "El" circled a portion of downtown Chicago.

Still, corruption proved more enduring than the reform movement. In the 1916 mayoral election, Chicago elected William "Big Bill" Thompson, a jovial but hopelessly corrupt politician, to replace the upright Harrison Carter, Jr. The reform movement dwindled.

ANOTHER WAR

In 1917 the United States entered World War I, joining Britain and France in war against Germany and its allies. Illinois sent over 300,000 men to the army and navy, many of them from its large population of German immigrants. Thousands of sailors passed through the Great Lakes Naval Training Center just north of Chicago. Nearby Fort Sheridan trained army officers. At Chanute field—named for an Illinois engineer who had been the Wright brothers' leading adviser—pilots trained for aerial combat. Illinois factories recruited thousands of blacks from the South to help produce a flood of weapons and supplies.

Reinvigorated with American troops, the Allied armies swept to victory in 1918. Illinois welcomed its service people home from "the war to end all wars" with wild celebration. Ahead lay the 1920s and Illinois's second century of statehood. Who could doubt that Illinois stood at the threshold of a remarkable era?

Upton Sinclair, author of The Jungle,
a book that helped pass legislation
regulating the quality of consumer products

BIG DREAMS AND
DIRTY POLITICS

Big, rowdy Chicago seemed perfectly suited to the "Roaring Twenties"—a decade remembered for its great optimism, its colorful, brutal gangsters, its speakeasies and jazz, and above all else, its unrestrained sense of fun. Of course, these romantic images ignore much that was humdrum about the twenties. Still, there is some truth in the romantic view—it *was* an exciting era, and nowhere was it more exciting than in Chicago.

PROHIBITION

The decade opened with a disastrous attempt to legislate morality. On January 29, 1920, the Eighteenth Amendment to the United States Constitution went into effect. The Prohibition Amendment outlawed all commercial production, sale, and consumption of alcoholic beverages. Tens of millions chose to ignore the rules. Prohibition would undermine respect for law and give organized crime a gold mine of opportunities.

Organized crime in Chicago dated back to the 1870s. In the twentieth century's late-teens, it thrived as Mayor Big Bill Thompson looked the other way. In 1919 a hefty young Italian from New York City, Alphonse Capone, arrived to help his friend Johnny Torrio take over Chicago's booming business in extortion, gambling, prostitution, loan-sharking, and other assorted crimes. Cunning and ruthless, Capone would soon dominate the Chicago underworld.

Torrio and Capone had rivals. In 1924 a mob war erupted. Torrio decided New York City was safer and left "Scarface" Al Capone to run Chicago. The war raged for several years with the death toll exceeding two hundred mobsters. On St. Valentine's Day, 1929, the gang war produced its most famous incident when hoodlums—probably Capone's—machine-gunned six members of George "Bugsie" Moran's gang and an unlucky bystander in a North Side garage.

The authorities never succeeded in pinning any of the era's bloody crimes on Capone. In 1931 he went to prison on tax-evasion charges. He was released in 1939, his mind and body destroyed by syphilis. Organized crime continued, and still plagues Chicago and other parts of Illinois.

THE GOOD LIFE

During Prohibition, otherwise law-abiding citizens thought little of patronizing one of Chicago's approximately twenty thousand speakeasies—so named because a reference or well-phrased request got a customer by the bouncer who inspected visitors through a sliding window in the door. Having a drink was part of the good life. As long as the average citizen used a little caution, Chicago was no more dangerous than any other big city.

Never before had most Illinoisans enjoyed such a high quality of life. The rates of child mortality and death from disease had dropped sharply from nineteenth-century levels. Incomes were up, and the average family could buy more luxuries than ever before—an electric refrigerator, a vacuum cleaner, a radio, even an automobile and a suburban home. A shortened work week gave people more time to enjoy life. Entertainment possibilities multiplied. Chicago—now a city of three million—had twenty-three theaters, great museums and libraries, a symphony, and hundreds of movie houses. Smaller cities had less to offer, but even a small town usually had a library, a movie house, and a local band.

Not everyone enjoyed the good life, however. Slums and grim conditions existed in Chicago, Peoria, East St. Louis, and other industrial cities. The immigration of blacks from the South sparked race riots, and unrest in the coal fields brought bloody confrontations. However, the general feeling was that the growing economy would eventually improve everyone's lot and promote social harmony.

Although government was often wasteful and tainted with corruption, it seemed to get the important things done. Public services improved and road paving continued at a furious rate. Airport construction was a new priority. Four airlines were flying into Chicago by 1926, and many smaller cities were building airports.

Illinois's rural residents shared in the good life of the 1920s. The use of tractors, insecticides, herbicides, and hybrid seed produced huge increases in farm production. Profitable soybeans replaced wheat as Illinois's most important crop after corn. Farmers spent their higher incomes on better equipment and home conveniences. For the first time, many rural families could afford an automobile, electricity, and a telephone.

THE CHICAGO RENAISSANCE

The energy of the era could be seen in Illinois's flourishing art world. Chicago had attracted talented artists since well before World War I. By the 1920s, "the Chicago Renaissance" was in full swing. The novelists H. B. Fuller, Ben Hecht, and Theodore Dreiser; the short-story master Sherwood Anderson; and the poets Vachel Lindsay, Edgar Lee Masters, and Carl Sandburg produced breakthroughs in American writing. One of their major concerns was the effect of industrialization and a rapidly changing world on common people. In Chicago, they were eye-to-eye with not only the problems but also the glory of the robust and unsentimental future.

THE GREAT DEPRESSION

For a while, it seemed that the good times would go on forever. However, the economic success of the 1920s was built on a shaky foundation of stock speculation and risky banking practices. On

"Black Thursday," October 24, 1929, a selling panic on the stock market touched off a wave of business and bank closings. In a few months, the nation found itself in the worst economic slump in its history. The Great Depression would last a decade, bringing suffering to tens of millions.

Once-thriving Illinois was a bleak place by 1933. In Chicago, industrial employment had fallen 50 percent and payrolls 75 percent. A million and a half Illinoisans were unemployed, and many more worked only part-time. Mortgage foreclosures had taken the homes and farms of tens of thousands. Samuel Insull's utilities empire had collapsed, wiping out the investments of over a million stock and bond holders, many of whom had invested their life savings. Bank closings had ruined the financial security of hundreds of thousands more.

City and state governments fought desperately to provide relief for the hungry, homeless, and despairing, but lacked enough money. Chicago was nearly bankrupt, and the state not much better off.

THE DEMOCRATS TAKE OFFICE

The Republican party received much of the blame for the Depression. In Chicago, Anton J. Cermak built a powerful Democratic organization heavily dependent on patronage, union and minority support, and rigorous party discipline. Although often attacked by reformers, the "machine" provided good wages to its patronage workers and good municipal services to the citizenry. The local ward captain provided ready access to government, and many people—

Anton J. Cermak (left) with Franklin Roosevelt. Cermak built the Democratic Party into a powerful organization in Chicago.

particularly in the working class—felt an intense loyalty to the machine.

The Democratic machine ended the era of Big Bill Thompson and secured the election of Cermak as mayor and Henry Horner as governor. Cermak would die of an assassin's bullet in 1933, but the machine's hold on Chicago would not weaken until the 1970s.

The Democratic resurgence in Illinois helped elect Franklin D. Roosevelt president in 1932. Roosevelt called for the repeal of Prohibition and instituted the New Deal, a program of massive public spending to revive the economy. New Deal agencies put millions to work. One hundred thousand Illinoisans between the ages of seventeen and twenty-three joined the Civilian Conservation Corps (CCC), providing muscle for numerous conservation projects across the country. The Works Projects Administration (WPA) employed an average of 200,000 Illinoisans between 1935 and 1940 to build bridges, roads, schools, airports, sewers, playgrounds, and much more. The Rural Electrification Administration (REA) brought electricity to thousands of remote Illinois farms.

The federal and state governments worked together on programs to provide old-age assistance, aid to dependent children, unemployment insurance, mortgage refinancing, soil conservation, crop price stabilization, and banking reform. Slowly, the economy began to recover.

WORLD WAR II
AND THE ATOM BOMB

In 1939 World War II broke out in Europe. The United States entered the war in 1941. Over a million Illinoisans served in the armed forces during the war. Hundreds of thousands of recruits were trained at Illinois bases.

On the home front, women joined the labor force in vast numbers, many filling jobs once thought too difficult for women. Blacks from the South arrived in large numbers to help fill the employment gap. Chicago added 20,000 Japanese-American refugees from the West Coast to its already diverse population.

Illinois became a major manufacturer of war materials. In Chicago alone, $1.3 billion was spent on war plants for producing aircraft engines, radios, radar equipment, torpedo components, and hundreds of other military items. The small town of Seneca on the Illinois River built landing craft. Giant arsenals at Rock Island, East Alton, Kankakee, Dixon, Springfield, and Marion produced explosives, bullets, artillery pieces, and machine guns. The farms of the Prairie State became more mechanized as farmers worked to produce more food. About 90 percent of Illinois's land was under cultivation, a record unequaled by any other state.

At the University of Chicago, scientists worked on a super-secret project that was to end the war and change the course of history. Their goal was to set off a nuclear chain reaction in the atoms of uranium. Uncontrolled, the chain reaction would produce a gigantic release of energy—the biggest bomb the world had ever known.

Under the direction of Dr. Enrico Fermi, the scientists succeeded in producing a controlled chain reaction in 1942. Their accomplishment led to the design of the world's first nuclear weapons. The United States used two atom bombs to force Japan's surrender in the summer of 1945.

STABLE GROWTH

Despite fears, the Depression did not reappear with the end of the war. Illinois enjoyed renewed prosperity in an era of stable growth. The state's population increased from 8.7 million in 1950 to 11.4 million in 1980, the fifth largest in the United States. The population of Chicago declined from 3.6 million to 3 million in the same period, but the loss was more than offset by the skyrocketing growth of the city's suburbs.

The real income of Illinois citizens increased dramatically in the postwar years. By the 1950s Illinoisans, on the average, enjoyed one of the highest standards of living in the world. Much of the growth in real income could be credited to the success of the unions.

Higher incomes allowed Illinoisans to buy more homes, cars, and appliances. Most of the new homes—often purchased with a veteran's loan—were in the suburbs, since increased automobile ownership gave more families the freedom to choose where they wanted to live. Eventually, the suburbs would have a higher population than the cities themselves.

PUBLIC EDUCATION

After World War II, Illinois modernized its educational system. Hundreds of one-room schools with teachers only slightly older and better educated than their students were replaced by modern schools with highly professional staffs. A high school diploma became a standard requirement for many jobs. More high school graduates went on to college than ever before.

Increased state funding made the Illinois public university system one of the nation's best. Two private schools, the University of Chicago and Northwestern University, earned international recognition.

TURBULENT POLITICS

Illinois's tradition of turbulent politics continued. The state contributed some exceptional leaders to the nation. Adlai Stevenson served as governor, ran twice as the Democratic presidential nominee, and

Richard J. Daley was
one of Chicago's most
controversial mayors.

became a noted statesman. Republican senator Everett Dirksen became Senate minority leader and one of the country's leading orators.

More controversial was Chicago's Mayor Richard J. Daley, for nearly twenty years one of the nation's most powerful politicians. Calling Chicago "the city that works," Daley not so much administered as ruled the giant city. His power lay with the Democratic machine and its vast network of patronage. And, despite inner-city problems of poverty, racial unrest, crime, and social decay, Chicago did seem to work better than most large American cities.

CIVIL RIGHTS CRUSADE

Chicago's rapidly growing population of blacks felt that Daley's administration paid little attention to their demands for equality in voting, housing, jobs, and government services. While downtown thrived, conditions in the slums deteriorated. The first of several "long, hot summers" of racial tension began in 1964.

In 1968 the assassination of the civil-rights leader Dr. Martin Luther King, Jr., touched off huge riots in Chicago, East St. Louis, Alton, Joliet, and dozens of cities in other states. Mayor Daley was widely criticized for ordering the Chicago police to shoot arsonists and looters. The National Guard and federal troops finally restored order in Chicago, but only after rioting had caused nine deaths, five hundred injuries, and three thousand arrests.

THE MACHINE WEAKENS

A few weeks later, the Democratic National Convention met in Chicago. The situation was tense as thousands gathered to protest the war in Vietnam. On the fourth night of the convention, Chicago police attacked thousands of marchers in what a federal commission would later call "a police riot."

Illinois National Guardsmen patrolling riot-wrecked streets after the assassination of Martin Luther King, Jr., touched off riots in many cities in Illinois as well as throughout the nation.

That night was a public relations disaster for Chicago and, particularly, its mayor. Most Democrats never forgave Daley. At their convention in 1972, the Democrats refused to seat the Illinois delegation headed by Daley. A reform delegation led by a liberal alderman took its place.

Defiant and bitter, Daley continued to rule Chicago until his death in 1976. Without Daley at the controls, the machine lost power. The interim mayor was defeated in 1979 by Jane Byrne, who became the city's first woman mayor. Byrne failed to restore the machine's power and was defeated in 1983 by Harold Washington, who became Chicago's first black mayor.

State government too was changing in the 1970s. A massive scandal led to calls for genuine reform. Daniel Walker won the governorship in 1972 by denouncing Daley and calling for clean government. In 1976 he was succeeded by James R. Thompson, a Republican who had made his reputation as a prosecutor.

CHICAGO'S SURGE OF GROWTH

In the 1970s many of Chicago's traditional industries such as steelmaking and railroading declined. Over 200,000 blue-collar jobs were lost, and many people were pessimistic about the city's future. However, the 1980s brought a surge of growth as finance, high technology, and other service and light industries boomed. Chicago's downtown underwent the largest renovation since the great fire of 1871. From 1979 to 1986, $6.8 billion was spent on construction in the 1,000-block city core. The city's office space doubled and

Police and anti-Vietnam War demonstrators battle during the Democratic National Convention in Chicago in 1968.

Mayor Harold Washington,
Chicago's first black mayor

17,300 housing units were added. Another $7.5 billion worth of construction was planned for the near future.

Like all large cities, Chicago had problems: traffic congestion, crime and drug abuse, slums, a large number of homeless residents, and aging bridges, streets, and sewers. Yet, "the city that works" was working overtime to build its future.

As Illinois looks toward the twenty-first century, it faces both problems and opportunities. States in the West and Southwest are growing faster, and—like other mature industrial states in the Midwest and Northeast—Illinois must adjust to new economic realities. However, its geographical position is as important as ever, its farms produce bumper harvests year after year, and its work force is among the most skilled and productive in the world. With those assets, Illinois's future is bright.

DYNAMO OF THE
HEARTLAND

Illinois today remains the economic dynamo of the Midwest. Fourth in total economic output among the states, Illinois ranks at or near the top in production of numerous industrial and agricultural products. Amid the prosperity, there are also problems. Like other mature industrial states, Illinois lags behind some southern and western states in growth. Unemployment is high, government services strained, and the future of important industries in doubt. Illinois's record of achievement is long, but new challenges lie ahead.

POPULATION

The 1980 census ranked Illinois fifth in the nation with a population of 11,426,518 in 4.2 million households. Growth in the previous ten years had been slight—about 312,000—and some population experts predicted that Illinois could see a significant decline in population by the end of the century.

Of the total population, about 9.23 million were white, about 1.68 million black, and about 500,000 Illinoisans declared other racial backgrounds. Most numerous in this latter group were Chinese, Filipinos, Japanese, Hispanics, Koreans, Vietnamese, and Asian Indians. Since the census, the Hispanic population has grown the fastest. A small number of American Indians also live in Illinois, but there are no known descendants of the Iliniwek.

In 1980 over 83 percent of Illinois people lived in urban areas. Chicago dwarfed all other urban areas with a population of just over 3 million in the city itself and 7.1 million in the metropolitan area.

The other cities with metropolitan areas over 100,000 were Rockford, 279,514 (city, 139,712); Peoria, 365,864 (city, 124,160); Springfield, 176,089 (city, 99,637); and Decatur, 131,375 (city, 94,081).

EMPLOYMENT

A 1984 survey of employment in Illinois recorded over 4.6 million people employed in nonagricultural industries. The categories measured were wholesale and retail trade, 1.14 million; services, 1.05 million; manufacturing, 986,000; government, 691,000; finance, insurance, and real estate, 318,000; transportation and public utilities, 274,000; and construction, 150,000.

The average annual pay of workers was $19,733 in 1984, comfortably above the national average of $18,350. However, Illinois had dropped from seventh to ninth place among the states in only four years. Illinois's unemployment rate of 9.1 percent was one of the highest in the country.

Unemployment in poorer neighborhoods of Chicago and other large industrial cities is much higher than the state average. Much of Illinois's huge welfare budget—the fifth highest in the nation—is spent keeping inner-city families afloat. A 1979 survey found 1.2 million Illinoisans living below the poverty line, including nearly 15 percent of its children. Only four other states had a higher poverty rate.

MANUFACTURING

Although sales and service industries now employ more workers, manufacturing remains vital to the Illinois economy. Major industries

Chicago's dramatic skyline

—77

include machinery, chemicals, electric and electronic equipment, steel, and food-processing. In 1982 about 18,600 manufacturing establishments were operating in the state. With a large union membership, Illinois workers earned almost a dollar per hour above the national average.

Illinois industry faces significant problems. Many factories are old and inefficient. Other states offer cheaper labor and energy costs. Foreign competition has hurt such basic industries as steel and machinery. Particularly vulnerable are smaller cities that depend on one major industry. Peoria's economy was recently devastated by massive layoffs at its giant Caterpillar machinery plant. Manufacturing employment in Illinois has fallen steadily in recent years and seems unlikely to rebound fully. Once-powerful unions are scrambling to find new ways to protect their members.

MINING

Illinois continues to be a national leader in several types of mining. Coal production is by far the most important. In 1980, sixty-one mines produced 61.4 million tons of coal worth $2.8 billion, giving Illinois fifth place among coal-producing states. In addition, Illinois ranked first in fluorspar, fourth in peat, and fourth in stone.

Mining in Illinois will provide a steady source of income for the foreseeable future. Coal production could increase significantly if cost-effective methods can be found to reduce the sulfur content of the state's coal.

AGRICULTURE

The farms of Illinois continue to be among the most productive in the world. In 1984 the state ranked third in the nation in total value of agricultural production. Illinois's first crop—which it has been since the beginning—is corn, with a 1984 harvest of 1.247 billion bushels. Only Iowa produced more, and all other states were far

*Manufacturing, such as the production of tractors,
has declined in the state in recent years.*

behind. Illinois ranked first in soybeans in 1984 with a harvest of 289 million bushels. The wheat harvest was 70.4 million bushels, good enough for thirteenth place. In addition to cash crops, Illinois raises large numbers of animals. A 1984 report estimated that Illinois had 5.4 million hogs (second in the nation), 2.5 million beef cattle (fifteenth), 225,000 milk cows (eleventh), and 136,000 sheep (seventeenth).

There are problems down on the farm. Illinois farmers face high equipment, energy, and chemical costs, uncertain market prices, and a heavy debt load. The trend is toward bigger, more efficient farms. In the first half of the 1980s, the number of farms dropped from some 107,000 to about 90,000. Total farmland remained at approximately 29 million acres (11,750,000 hectares), while the size of the average farm increased from 269 to 322 acres (109 to 130 hectares).

The changing nature of Illinois farming has produced a dramatic decline in the farming population. Between 1960 and 1980, the farming population plunged from 621,000 to 314,000. That trend continues, and today less than 2.75 percent of the state's people live on farms.

GOVERNMENT

Illinois politics are probably cleaner today than they have been in generations. Illinoisans turn out at the polls in numbers well above the national average. In recent years, Democrats have held majorities in both houses of the legislature, while Governor Thompson has kept the statehouse in Republican hands. The state usually sends more Democrats than Republicans to Congress, but has voted for Republican presidential candidates since 1968. Blacks and women do well with Illinois voters in local and state elections.

In 1983 state and local governments spent $21.8 billion, the fourth highest total in the nation. However, the expense was divided many ways, and Illinois ranked seventeenth in taxes paid by indi-

*Agriculture is an important
industry in Illinois.*

viduals. State debt was low and the finances of most municipalities sound.

TRANSPORTATION

Maintaining and expanding Illinois's vast transportation system is a major expense for government. In 1983 Illinois had approximately 130,000 miles (209,000 km) of road. Illinoisans owned close to 6 million cars, over a million trucks and buses, and some 230,000 motorcycles. The state had 125 public airports, and the privately run railroad system of over 10,000 miles (16,000 km) was one of the finest in the world.

In 1959 completion of the Saint Lawrence Seaway made Chicago an international port. In 1981 the port handled 31.6 million tons of cargo. However, competition from rail and trucking firms has dimmed the prospects of "America's fourth seacoast" and its largest port.

EDUCATION

More of Illinois taxpayers' money is spent on education than any other item. The state has about 4,450 public schools. In 1983, 1,271,525 students attended elementary schools and 581,791 were enrolled in secondary schools. The spending per student was about $3,500 a year, slightly above the national average.

Illinois also supported sixty-three institutions of higher education with a total enrollment of over half a million in 1983. The largest of the state-supported universities were the University of Illinois–Urbana (about 65,000 students), the University of Southern Illinois at

The state is a major supplier of corn.

—83

Carbondale (about 35,000), Northern Illinois University at De Kalb (about 26,000), and Illinois State University at Normal (about 20,000).

Students could also choose among 1,300 private elementary and secondary schools and 97 private colleges and universities. The largest private university is Northwestern in Evanston, with approximately 16,000 students in 1983.

The educational level of Illinois residents is close to national averages. About two-thirds of its residents have high school degrees, around 31 percent have some higher education, and about 16 percent are college graduates.

TOURISM IN ILLINOIS

The Prairie State offers a large number of recreational opportunities. In 1984 out-of-state visitors spent $6.2 billion in Illinois, making tourism a major industry.

The great city of Chicago attracts visitors from all over the world. Chicago is a showplace for modern architecture. The 109-story Sears Tower is the world's tallest building at 1,468 feet (447 m). Seventeen thousand employees work in its 129,000 square feet (11,985 sq m). The nearby Standard Oil Building is the world's fourth tallest building at 1,136 feet (346 m). At the top of North Michigan Avenue—"the magnificent mile" of luxury shops and high-priced developments—is the Hancock Center, the world's largest combined office and apartment building and the world's fifth tallest building at 1,100 feet (335 m).

There are other world recordholders in the business district. The Chicago Board of Trade is the world's largest grain exchange. The Merchandise Mart is the world's biggest wholesale center. Mc-Cormick Place on Lake Michigan is the world's largest exhibition hall and convention center with an incredible 1,078,000 square feet (100,150 sq m).

Chicago has some of the world's great museums including the Field Museum of Natural History, the Museum of Science and Industry, the Oriental Institute at the University of Chicago, the Museum of Contemporary Art, and the Art Institute of Chicago. Chicago's ethnic roots are featured at the DuSable Museum of Afro-American History, the Polish Museum (Chicago has more people of Polish ancestry than any city in the world except Warsaw), and smaller ethnic museums.

The wonders of nature are on display at the Lincoln Park Zoo, the Shedd Aquarium, and the Adler Planetarium. Garfield Park Conservatory's four and a half acres of flowers and plants make it one of the world's largest indoor gardens.

Chicago's historic sites include: Jane Addams's Hull House; the Water Tower (one of the few structures that survived the 1871 fire); Old Town with its restored Victorian homes; the Rookery and other early skyscrapers; and the Prairie Avenue Historic District, a former "millionaires' row" of mansions.

EXPLORING ILLINOIS

The Prairie State has much to offer outside Chicago, including dozens of picturesque towns and historic sites. Illinois's 382,000 acres (154,710 hectares) of state and federal forests, wildlife refuges, and parks attracted over 31 million visitors in 1984. It is impossible to list all of Illinois's attractions in a few pages, but the tourist may want to add a few of the following to the itinerary.

Near Chicago, Lockport was once the headquarters of the famous canal and today features historic buildings and four locks within the town. In the northwest corner of the state, Galena's lead-mining heritage is preserved in its old houses, including the home grateful citizens presented to General Ulysses S. Grant. The Galena area also has some of the state's most beautiful scenery.

The motorist can drive south from Galena along the Great River Road running beside the Mississippi. A short detour to the east will bring the visitor to Tampico, the childhood home of President Ronald Reagan. At Rock Island, the tourist can visit the huge army arsenal,

Illinois conservation officers displaying fish.
The state is trying to clean up its environment.

which includes buildings used in the Civil War for producing ammunition and safeguarding prisoners of war.

Further down the river is the historic town of Nauvoo where the Mormons built a bustling community from 1839 to 1846. Their controversial beliefs attracted many enemies, and nearby Carthage preserves the site where the Mormon prophet Joseph Smith and his brother were killed by a mob in 1844.

The city of Quincy is a good point to turn east for a tour of Lincoln country. New Salem, where Lincoln spent his young manhood clerking in a store and studying law, has been reconstructed by the state. In Springfield, the state capital, the National Park Service is restoring the neighborhood where Lincoln lived and practiced law before his election to the presidency. Lincoln's Tomb is on the outskirts of town.

A drive of less than two hours to the southwest brings the motorist to the outskirts of East St. Louis and Cahokia Mounds Historic Site with its spectacular earthworks left by the Middle Mississippian civilization. Continuing south to Chester, the traveler drives through American Bottom, where the French and the first English-speaking pioneers settled in Illinois. Fort de Chartres Historic Site preserves many memories of the early days in Illinois. A few miles further south is Kaskaskia, the only town in Illinois on the west side of the Mississippi. Unfortunately, visitors hoping to find the site of the state's first capital will be disappointed to learn that it was swept away by floods in 1881.

As the motorist continues south toward the tip of Illinois, level farmland gives way to rolling hills and valleys. In the "Illinois Ozarks," Shawnee National Forest offers 211,000 acres (85,460 hectares) for outdoor recreation. Nearby Crab Orchard National Wildlife Refuge sets aside 43,000 acres (17,400 hectares) for the conservation of animals and migratory birds.

Historic Cairo, Illinois's southernmost city, stands on a narrow tongue of land between the Ohio and Mississippi rivers. After walking about the picturesque town and visiting beautiful Magnolia Manor,

*Abraham Lincoln's house in Springfield
was the only home he ever owned.*

the visitor will want to see Fort Defiance State Park. From the site of the old Civil War fort, there is a magnificent view of the two great rivers joining to flow south toward Memphis and New Orleans.

On the banks of the great rivers, the traveler may well reflect on the long history of the Prairie State. From that distant time when Paleo-Indians first saw Illinois, its richness has drawn men and women from afar. Some cultures have grown, thrived, and fallen away, but other people have always arrived in pursuit of new dreams. Today the state has a population of immense diversity and talent. Illinois faces challenges in its maturity as it did in its earliest days. Yet, in its striving to build a better tomorrow, Illinois remains as youthful as ever.

FOR FURTHER READING

Cromie, Robert. *A Short History of Chicago*. San Francisco: Lexikos, 1984.

Howard, Robert P. *Illinois: A History of the Prairie State*. Grand Rapids, Mich.: W. B. Eerdmans, 1972.

Jensen, Richard J. *Illinois: A Bicentennial History*. New York: W. W. Norton, 1978.

Naden, Corinne J. *The Chicago Fire*. New York: Franklin Watts, 1969.

Nelson, Ronald E., ed., *Illinois: Land and Life in the Prairie State*. Dubuque, Iowa: Kendall/Hunt, 1978.

INDEX

ABOUT THE AUTHOR

Alden R. Carter is a versatile writer for children and young adults. He has written nonfiction books on electronics, supercomputers, radio, and the People's Republic of China. His novels *Growing Season* (1984) and *Wart, Son of Toad* (1985) were named to the American Library Association's annual list of best books for young adults. His most recent novel is *Sheila's Dying*. He is currently preparing a four-volume history of the American Revolution for Franklin Watts. Mr. Carter lives with his wife, Carol, and their son, Brian Patrick, in Marshfield, Wisconsin.

8   6/20/88